Instant Galleria How-to

Recipes to make you an expert user of the Galleria JavaScript framework

Nathan Van Gheem

PUBLISHING

BIRMINGHAM - MUMBAI

Instant Galleria How-to

Copyright © 2013 Packt Publishing

All rights reserved. No part of this book may be reproduced, stored in a retrieval system, or transmitted in any form or by any means, without the prior written permission of the publisher, except in the case of brief quotations embedded in critical articles or reviews.

Every effort has been made in the preparation of this book to ensure the accuracy of the information presented. However, the information contained in this book is sold without warranty, either express or implied. Neither the author, nor Packt Publishing, and its dealers and distributors will be held liable for any damages caused or alleged to be caused directly or indirectly by this book.

Packt Publishing has endeavored to provide trademark information about all of the companies and products mentioned in this book by the appropriate use of capitals. However, Packt Publishing cannot guarantee the accuracy of this information.

First published: February 2013

Production Reference: 1080213

Published by Packt Publishing Ltd.
Livery Place
35 Livery Street
Birmingham B3 2PB, UK.

ISBN 978-1-84969-660-9

www.packtpub.com

Credits

Author
Nathan Van Gheem

Reviewer
Victor Berchet

Acquisition Editor
Usha Iyer

Commissioning Editor
Ameya Sawant

Technical Editor
Kirti Pujari

Project Coordinator
Esha Thakker

Proofreader
Lawrence A. Herman

Production Coordinator
Conidon Miranda

Cover Work
Conidon Miranda

Cover Image
Conidon Miranda

About the Author

Nathan Van Gheem primarily works on Python web solutions. He also has extensive experience with JavaScript and integrating JavaScript solutions in web applications. He is involved with the Plone Python CMS open source community where he is the UI team leader and is on the Security team.

I would like to thank my family for the sacrifice of time they put up with, Wildcard Corp for giving me an opportunity to work on interesting projects, and Kim Nguyen for encouraging and enabling me to challenge myself with open source software.

About the Reviewer

Victor Berchet was introduced to web development in 2007 by playing with Google Maps, JavaScript API, and PHP, after having spent 10 years in the domain of embedded software development. He became a freelance Web Engineer in 2010 by founding Suumit, his own company. Most of the projects Victor works on involve either JavaScript mapping or the Symfony2 PHP framework. He is pretty much engaged in open source software and is one of the top contributors of Symfony2.

www.PacktPub.com

Support files, eBooks, discount offers and more

You might want to visit www.PacktPub.com for support files and downloads related to your book.

Did you know that Packt offers eBook versions of every book published, with PDF and ePub files available? You can upgrade to the eBook version at www.PacktPub.com and as a print book customer, you are entitled to a discount on the eBook copy. Get in touch with us at service@packtpub.com for more details.

At www.PacktPub.com, you can also read a collection of free technical articles, sign up for a range of free newsletters and receive exclusive discounts and offers on Packt books and eBooks.

http://PacktLib.PacktPub.com

Do you need instant solutions to your IT questions? PacktLib is Packt's online digital book library. Here, you can access, read and search across Packt's entire library of books.

Why Subscribe?

- ▸ Fully searchable across every book published by Packt
- ▸ Copy and paste, print and bookmark content
- ▸ On demand and accessible via web browser

Free Access for Packt account holders

If you have an account with Packt at www.PacktPub.com, you can use this to access PacktLib today and view nine entirely free books. Simply use your login credentials for immediate access.

Table of Contents

Preface

Galleria is a JavaScript framework for building beautiful image galleries for the web. It comes packed with responsive web design support and swipe for mobile devices. With its flexible theming system, you'll be able to customize it to your needs or you can use one of the many available themes. It is open sourced under the MIT license and comes packed with a free classic theme. Galleria has a large user base with many web application add-ons already provided on various platforms. It's an obvious choice for creating beautifully customized galleries on your website.

If you want to integrate Galleria to create your own beautiful image galleries for the web, Galleria How-to is the book you need.

Using concise recipes, Galleria How-to will take you from creating and configuring your first gallery to creating themes and plugins, using the Galleria API and integrating with web applications.

What this book covers

Setting up the development environment (Simple) details how to set up a development environment to start developing with Galleria.

Your first gallery (Simple) introduces creating a simple gallery.

Configuring Galleria (Simple) details how to configure Galleria with JavaScript and HTML attributes.

Installing themes (Simple) discusses how to install and use different themes.

Creating your own theme (Medium) details the process of creating custom themes with JavaScript and CSS.

Creating mobile friendly themes (Simple) introduces how to create mobile friendly themes using responsive web design.

Installing plugins (Simple) details how to install and use plugins.

Using the Flickr plugin (Medium) goes more in depth with using plugins by configuring and customizing the use of the flickr plugin.

Creating a plugin (Advanced) discusses in-depth how to create a plugin from scratch.

Using the API (Medium) details taking full control of Galleria's API to customize its behavior.

Alternative image data structures (Simple) explains how to use different data structures and mechanism to instruct Galleria on what images to use.

Optimizing Galleria (Simple) introduces how to improve your gallery and website performance.

Adding images dynamically (Medium) explains how to use JavaScript to incrementally add images to galleries.

Triggering Galleria (Advanced) details triggering Galleria from events outside of the gallery.

Recording image views with Google Analytics (Medium) details how to track hits on images in galleries to improve analytics.

Handling errors gracefully (Medium) explains how to handle gracefully potential problems that could arise with Galleria.

Creating tests for customizations (Advanced) discusses creating tests on customizations for quality assurance.

Web application integration (Advanced) details how to integrate Galleria with web applications using a simple example in Python.

What you need for this book

To follow the recipes in this book, you will need a computer suitable for developing JavaScript, HTML, and CSS. You may use Windows, Mac OS X, or Linux. You will need a modern web browser with debugging tools such as Mozilla Firefox or Google Chrome, and a text editor.

We will cover setting up a development environment, including downloading of the Galleria source code, in the first recipe of this book, *Setting up the development environment.*

Who this book is for

This book assumes the reader is comfortable reading and editing JavaScript, HTML, and CSS. With a basic understanding of JavaScript, most of the book is very applicable. An in-depth understanding of HTML and CSS is required throughout the book.

Conventions

In this book, you will find a number of styles of text that distinguish between different kinds of information. Here are some examples of these styles, and an explanation of their meaning.

Code words in text are shown as follows: "We can include other contexts through the use of the `include` directive."

A block of code is set as follows:

```
$(document).ready(function(){
  Galleria.loadTheme(
    '../themes/classic/galleria.classic.min.js');
  Galleria.run('#galleria');
});
```

When we wish to draw your attention to a particular part of a code block, the relevant lines or items are set in bold:

```
Galleria.configure({
    autoplay: true
});
```

Any command-line input or output is written as follows:

```
# cp /usr/src/asterisk-addons/configs/cdr_mysql.conf.sample
    /etc/asterisk/cdr_mysql.conf
```

New terms and **important words** are shown in bold. Words that you see on the screen, in menus or dialog boxes for example, appear in the text like this: "clicking the **Next** button moves you to the next screen."

 Warnings or important notes appear in a box like this.

 Tips and tricks appear like this.

Reader feedback

Feedback from our readers is always welcome. Let us know what you think about this book—what you liked or may have disliked. Reader feedback is important for us to develop titles that you really get the most out of.

To send us general feedback, simply send an e-mail to `feedback@packtpub.com`, and mention the book title via the subject of your message.

If there is a topic that you have expertise in and you are interested in either writing or contributing to a book, see our author guide on `www.packtpub.com/authors`.

Customer support

Now that you are the proud owner of a Packt book, we have a number of things to help you to get the most from your purchase.

Downloading the example code

You can download the example code files for all Packt books you have purchased from your account at `http://www.PacktPub.com`. If you purchased this book elsewhere, you can visit `http://www.PacktPub.com/support` and register to have the files e-mailed directly to you.

Errata

Although we have taken every care to ensure the accuracy of our content, mistakes do happen. If you find a mistake in one of our books—maybe a mistake in the text or the code—we would be grateful if you would report this to us. By doing so, you can save other readers from frustration and help us improve subsequent versions of this book. If you find any errata, please report them by visiting `http://www.packtpub.com/support`, selecting your book, clicking on the **errata submission form** link, and entering the details of your errata. Once your errata are verified, your submission will be accepted and the errata will be uploaded on our website, or added to any list of existing errata, under the Errata section of that title. Any existing errata can be viewed by selecting your title from `http://www.packtpub.com/support`.

Piracy

Piracy of copyright material on the Internet is an ongoing problem across all media. At Packt, we take the protection of our copyright and licenses very seriously. If you come across any illegal copies of our works, in any form, on the Internet, please provide us with the location address or website name immediately so that we can pursue a remedy.

Please contact us at copyright@packtpub.com with a link to the suspected pirated material.

We appreciate your help in protecting our authors, and our ability to bring you valuable content.

Questions

You can contact us at questions@packtpub.com if you are having a problem with any aspect of the book, and we will do our best to address it.

Galleria How-to

Welcome to Galleria How-to. This How-to will guide you to become an expert at utilizing the Galleria gallery framework to make beautiful and functional galleries for websites that scale to mobile platforms.

Setting up the development environment (Simple)

This section will cover how to get prepared to start developing with Galleria. We'll install and run Galleria with the classic theme, create the folder structure, and set up the development environment.

Getting ready

Before we start developing with Galleria, you'll need a text editor to use throughout this book since we'll be modifying HTML, JavaScript, and CSS.

How to do it...

1. First, you'll need to download the Galleria source code. In a web browser, visit `http://galleria.io/download` and download the latest Galleria source code. At the time this book was written, Galleria was at Version 1.2.8.

2. Once the download is finished, extract it, and inspect the contents of the download.

3. We'll then add a new folder in the previous extracted source and name it `development`. This is where we'll do all our Galleria development for the rest of the book.

4. Inside the `development` directory, we'll then create an `images` folder. Please insert test images in this folder to use with the development galleries we'll create.

5. Once done, the contents of the Galleria source should look like the following screenshot:

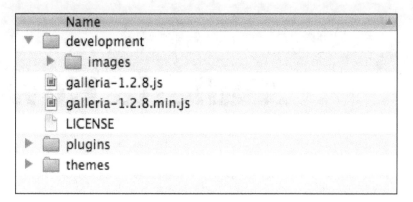

6. Next, let's test whether the downloaded Galleria source code is working properly or not. Galleria comes with a free default theme called "classic". Navigate to `themes/classic/classic-demo.html` and open the file in a modern web browser (Google Chrome, Firefox, or Microsoft Internet Explorer version 8 or later), which should result in the following gallery:

Galleria components

Here, we'll cover that part of Galleria that provides the gallery functionality.

- ► `galleria.js`: This is the gallery script that loads images and facilitates the gallery functionality.

- ► `theme javascript`: A theme consists of a combination of JavaScript, HTML, and CSS to provide a unique load and feel.

- ► `plugins`: These plugins are used to extend and override the way `galleria.js` works. For instance, there is a `flickr` plugin to get images from flickr and not from the HTML DOM as that is used frequently.

If you don't have a text editor...

There are many great open source text editors that you can use to edit HTML, JavaScript, and CSS. For Windows, Notepad++ is a great text editor. It can be found at `http://notepad-plus-plus.org/`. For Mac OS X, TextWrangler is a very good free text editor that can be found at `http://www.barebones.com/products/TextWrangler/`.

You are also free to use the default text editors that come with your operating system but they're usually not as easy to use for development.

Extracting the source code

The Galleria source code download will come in a zipped archive format that is extractable on most modern operating systems. If you have trouble extracting the source code for Windows, use 7zip, available at `http://www.7-zip.org/`. Mac OS X should be able to extract all archive types you come across.

Your first gallery (Simple)

In this recipe, we're going to go through the basics of creating a Galleria gallery. HTML structure and Galleria JavaScript are topics that will be covered in this recipe.

Getting ready

Assemble together a group of images that you'll use while working with Galleria and place them into your Galleria development image source directory (`galleria/development/images`).

How to do it...

1. Create a `myfirstgallery.html` file inside the `development` folder.

2. Start off with the usual HTML5 doctype structure.

3. Inside the head section include the JavaScript dependencies, `jquery.js` and `galleria.js`. In both the cases, we'll use the following minified versions:

```
<!DOCTYPE html>
<html lang="en">
  <head>
    <script src="http://code.jquery.com/jquery.min.js">
    </script>
    <script src="../galleria-1.2.8.min.js"></script>
    /* end of Javascript file includes */
```

Make sure the relative path used to reference `galleria.js` is correct for the folder structure being used.

Downloading the example code

You can download the example code files for all Packt books you have purchased from your account at `http://www.PacktPub.com`. If you purchased this book elsewhere, you can visit `http://www.PacktPub.com/support` and register to have the files e-mailed directly to you.

4. Next, we'll need to provide the following code to initialize the gallery:

```
/* end of Javascript file includes */
<script>
$(document).ready(function(){
  Galleria.loadTheme(
    '../themes/classic/galleria.classic.min.js');
  Galleria.run('#galleria');
});
</script>
</head>
/* end of head tag */
```

- ❑ Here, `$(document).ready` is a jQuery construct used to run the code inside the anonymous function after the document is ready. This is important because we need to load the gallery after all the images are loaded in the DOM.

- ❑ The `Galleria.loadTheme` function loads the theme file. It takes only one parameter, the path of the JavaScript file.

- ❑ Finally, the `Galleria.run` function is used to wire a gallery up via a CSS selector. In this case, `#galleria` refers to a tag with the ID of "galleria" that we'll define later.

5. Next, we'll add references to the images we want to provide in the gallery. The standard way to do this, demonstrated here, is to provide them through an HTML structure. The basic structure is to provide the full size image as the `href` attribute of an anchor tag. The thumbnail image is defined via an `img` tag. If you have not generated thumbnails, just use your full size image for the thumbnail.

6. Inside the body tag, we'll provide the following HTML code to reference the images for our gallery:

```html
<body>
 <div id="galleria" style="height: 500px;">
   <a href="images/image1-1600px.jpg">
     <img data-title="Image 1"
          data-description="Image 1 description"
          src="images/image1-200px.jpg" />
   </a>
   <!-- Additional images in same HTML format
        can be provided below -->
 </div>
</body>
```

- ❑ The `id="galleria"` attribute and value refers to what we were using with the `Galleria.run` method to instruct Galleria where to look for the images

- ❑ The `style="height: 500px;"` attribute and value gives a height to the gallery, which is required for Galleria to function

- ❑ The `data-title` attribute is where we can give our image a title that the theme will use

- ❑ Finally, the `data-description` attribute, similar to the title attribute, gives the image a description to be shown in the gallery

How it works...

Galleria searches the `div` tag with the id `"galleria"` to find images to load the gallery. Galleria then calls the theme JavaScript initialization code to generate additional HTML and JavaScript events that set up the gallery further. Essentially, `galleria.js` provides the basic gallery components and the theme uses these components to further customize the look and feel of the gallery.

Defining a height

It is important to define a height for all Galleria galleries. If no height is defined in CSS or a style tag, the gallery will fail to load.

Data attributes

In this example, we use data attributes, which are attributes that start with "data-", to define the title and description of the image. We could have just as easily specified `title` and `alt` attributes that would also populate the title and description values. Either way works the same.

Configuring Galleria (Simple)

In this recipe, we'll learn how to get more out of Galleria by knowing how to turn the knobs that will customize the gallery in different ways.

Getting ready

In this example, please utilize the code we wrote in the first *How to do it...* section, or work with the `themes/classic/classic-demo.html` file. Both will allow us to manipulate configuration options.

How to do it...

To configure Galleria, we'll use the `Galleria.configure` method. This method accepts a JavaScript object of keys and values.

```
Galleria.configure({
    autoplay: true
});
```

In this example, we're invoking Galleria to automatically start the gallery when the page is loaded with the `autoplay` option.

How it works...

The JavaScript object passed into the `Galleria.configure` method overrides or extends the default Galleria configuration. This configuration is then passed on to the theme loaded and plugins that are installed.

There's more...

We can also combine the `Galleria.run` method call with configuration options. Using the example we've been working with, the `Galleria.run` method call would look as follows:

```
Galleria.run('#galleria', {autoplay: true});
```

Useful configuration options

Here, we'll cover the most useful Galleria configuration options.

- ▶ `autoplay`: This option automatically starts the gallery on page load. Its default value is set to false.

- ▶ `carousel`: This option controls whether a carousel is created. Its default value is set to true.

- ▶ `carouselSpeed`: This option controls the animation speed of changes in the carousel in milliseconds. Its default value is set to 200.

- ▶ `height`: This option manually sets the gallery height. This is useful if no height is set in CSS. Its default value is set to 0.

- ▶ `width`: This option manually sets the gallery width. This is useful if no width is set in CSS and constraining the gallery width is required. Its default value is set to 0.

- ▶ `transition`: This option customizes the transition used for changing images. It defaults to "fade" for most themes but is "slide" for the classic theme.

- ▶ `transitionSpeed`: This option customizes the duration of the transition. Its default value is set to 400 milliseconds.

- ▶ `preload`: This option provides the number of images to preload in the gallery. It defaults to 2.

- ▶ `responsive`: This option tells Galleria to resize when the window size changes. This will only work along with media queries that define how the gallery should look with different window sizes. Its default value is set to false.

- ▶ `show`: This option customizes which image should be displayed first. It defaults to 0 (first image).

- ▶ `showInfo`: This option shows the caption information. It defaults to true.

- ▶ `thumbnails`: This option customizes how the thumbnails are generated. The following are the possible values for this option:
    - ❑ `true`: This value shows thumbnail images
    - ❑ `false`: This value does not show the thumbnail browser
    - ❑ `"empty"`: This value places empty span tags with the class of "img"
    - ❑ `"numbers"`: This value places empty span tags with numbers instead of images

All of these options are also defined in the Galleria source code and on Galleria's website documentation.

Complete listing of options

Visit `http://galleria.io/docs/options/` for a complete listing of Galleria options.

Installing themes (Simple)

Installing different themes will allow us to give Galleria a different look and feel, and in this recipe we will explore how we can use themes and install them.

Getting ready

The theme we'll be working with is the classic theme that comes with the Galleria source code.

How to do it...

There are two ways by which we can load theme files into Galleria:

1. The first is to use the Galleria API to load the theme JavaScript file:

   ```
   Galleria.loadTheme('../themes/classic/galleria.classic.min.js');
   ```

   The only parameter the `loadTheme` function takes is a string that is the relative path to the theme JavaScript file.

2. The second way to load the theme JavaScript file is simply to include the JavaScript file via the `script` tag as follows:

   ```
   <script src="../themes/classic/galleria.classic.min.js">
   </script>
   ```

The theme JavaScript file needs to be loaded before the `Galleria.run` function in order to start Galleria with the theme loaded.

How it works...

The theme file will automatically load dependent CSS files required for the theme. It will additionally run initialization code for theme specific look and feel.

There's more...

It's possible to dynamically change Galleria themes by loading other themes with the `Galleria.loadTheme` function.

Downloading Galleria themes

Galleria only comes with one free theme, the **Classic** theme, which comes with the Galleria source code. Other themes can be found at `http://galleria.io/`.

As of the writing of this book, there are no other useful sources for themes for Galleria. Sparse references to themes can be found in some github projects and also in some CMS Galleria integration packages. However, it's not easy to know how to use these themes without some customization, so we won't cover them in this book.

Creating your own theme (Medium)

Creating your own theme will allow you to customize Galleria in a very simple format. Here we will also introduce the structure for creating a basic theme.

Getting ready

In order to keep all the theme related files together, create a new folder inside the development folder named `themes`. Within the new `themes` folder, create another folder named `basic`. After this is done, our folder structure should be identical to the following screenshot:

▼ 📁 development	Today 10:08 PM	--	Folder
▶ 📁 images	Today 10:07 PM	--	Folder
📄 myfirstgallery.html	Today 6:56 PM	2 KB	HTML...ument
▼ 📁 themes	Today 10:08 PM	--	Folder
▶ 📁 basic	Today 10:08 PM	--	Folder
📄 galleria-1.2.8.js	Aug 9, 2012 1:07 PM	180 KB	JavaScript
📄 galleria-1.2.8.min.js	Aug 9, 2012 1:07 PM	59 KB	JavaScript
📄 LICENSE	Aug 9, 2012 1:07 PM	1 KB	Document
▶ 📁 plugins	Apr 5, 2012 3:45 PM	--	Folder
▶ 📁 themes	Yesterday 4:40 PM	--	Folder

Lastly, create empty `galleria.basic.js`, `galleria.basic.css`, and `galleria.basic-example.html` files inside the `basic` folder that was just created. Then, copy the contents of the `myfirstgallery.html` file and insert the text into the `galleria.basic-example.html` file. These are the files that we will be customizing in this recipe.

How to do it...

1. First, let's create the skeleton for our basic galleria theme in the `galleria.basic.js` file:

```
(function($) {
Galleria.addTheme({
    name: 'basic',
    author: 'Galleria How-to',
    css: 'galleria.basic.css',
    defaults: { transition: 'slide' },
    init: function(options) {
    }
});
}(jQuery));
```

The `addTheme` function registers the theme with the provided settings to Galleria. The `.css` file specified with the `css` option is automatically loaded here also. The `init` anonymous function is empty right now but this is where we would put the custom JavaScript functionality.

2. Next, we'll go on to styling our gallery. At its basic level, this involves placing tags into the DOM so that they can be positioned on the page.

    The major components of the gallery that need to be styled are:

    -   `#galleria-loader`
    -   `.galleria-info`
    -   `.galleria-stage`
    -   `.galleria-thumbnails-container`
    -   `.galleria-counter`
    -   `.galleria-image-nav`

    Now, let's go through the contents of the CSS file that provides very basic styles for our gallery.

    ```
    #galleria{ height: 550px; }
    ```

The preceding code sets the height of the gallery. This is required by the gallery to load and scale all the elements for the gallery correctly.

```
#galleria-loader{height:1px!important}
```

The preceding code provides the definition of the gallery loader container that is required for Galleria to load properly.

```
.galleria-stage { position: absolute; top: 0;
  bottom: 60px; left: 10px; right: 10px;
  width: 500px; float: right; max-height: 550px;}
```

`.galleria-stage` is the container for the images, loader, counter, and gallery navigation buttons.

```
.galleria-thumbnails-container { top: 0;
  position: absolute; left: 10px; right: 10px;
  z-index: 2; width: 500px; }
```

`.galleria-thumbnails-container` is the container for the thumbnail carousel. Here, we're placing it on top of the gallery.

```
.galleria-thumbnails .galleria-image { height: 40px;
    width: 60px; margin: 0 5px 0 0;
    border: 1px solid #000;
    float: left; cursor: pointer; }
```

With this rule we're styling the images in the thumbnail carousel. We make sure to float left here so that the images are displayed one after another.

```
.galleria-info{ position: absolute; top: 48px; opacity: 0.7;
  background-color: #F1F1F1; z-index: 4; left: 10px;
  width: 500px; }
```

With this rule, we target the tag that places the title and description of the images as they're browsed. In this theme, we're placing it just below the thumbnail carousel.

```
.galleria-counter { position: absolute; bottom: 30px;
  left: 10px; }
```

`.galleria-counter` is used to display which image the user is currently viewing out of the total number of images in the gallery.

```
.galleria-image-nav { position: absolute; top: 50%;
    margin-top: -62px; width: 500px; height: 62px;
    left: 0; }
```

`.galleria-image-nav` places the navigation buttons on the gallery so that we can manually move forward and backward in the gallery. In this case, we're just trying to place the buttons in the middle of the gallery.

```
.galleria-image-nav-left,
.galleria-image-nav-right { opacity: .5; cursor: pointer;
   width: 35px; height: 124px; position: absolute;
   left: 0; z-index: 2; background-color: gray; }
.galleria-image-nav-right { left: auto; right: 0;
   z-index: 2;}
.galleria-image-nav-left:hover,
.galleria-image-nav-right:hover { opacity: .9; }
```

This preceding set of rules places right and left navigation buttons on the edges of the gallery.

3. Finally, we need to modify the inline JavaScript code in our `galleria.basic-example.html` file to call our new theme, using the following code:

```
<script src="http://code.jquery.com/jquery.min.js"></script>
<script src="../../../galleria-1.2.8.min.js"></script>
<script>
$(document).ready(function(){
  Galleria.loadTheme('galleria.basic.js');
     Galleria.run('#galleria');
});
</script>
```

4. Additionally, you'll need to change the image references in the `galleria-basic-example.html` file to work with the images where they are stored. If following along with the provided code and examples, the images should be placed two folders above the theme file:

```
<a href="../../images/image1-1600px.jpg">
  <img title="Image 1"
        alt="Image 1 description"
        src="../../images/image1-200px.jpg" />
</a>
```

This is essentially identical to our previous Galleria bootstrapping with the simple exception that we're loading the new `galleria.basic.js` theme instead of the classic theme in the following screenshot:

```
▼<div id="galleria" style="height: 500px;">
  ▼<div class="galleria-container notouch" style="width: 1901px; height: 500px;">
    ▼<div class="galleria-stage">
      ►<div class="galleria-images" style="position: relative; top: 0px; left: 0px; width: 100%; height: 100%;">…</div>
        <div class="galleria-loader"></div>
      ►<div class="galleria-counter" style="opacity: 1;">…</div>
      ►<div class="galleria-image-nav">…</div>
      </div>
    ▼<div class="galleria-thumbnails-container galleria-carousel">
        <div class="galleria-thumb-nav-left disabled"></div>
      ►<div class="galleria-thumbnails-list" style="overflow: hidden; position: relative;">…</div>
        <div class="galleria-thumb-nav-right"></div>
      </div>
    ▼<div class="galleria-info">
      ►<div class="galleria-info-text">…</div>
      </div>
      <div class="galleria-tooltip" style="opacity: 0;"></div>
    </div>
  </div>
```

Once finished, the theme should be rendering a screen like the following screenshot:

How it works...

Galleria loads the theme JavaScript file we specified in the `Galleria.loadTheme` function. Galleria then looks at the CSS file specified in the theme JavaScript file to load the stylesheets. The markup is generated by Galleria and then all the styling is done by us.

For the sake of brevity

The basic gallery is very plain and obviously doesn't look very appealing. This is so we don't get bombarded with too many CSS rules to digest. We're going to work with the most barebones examples possible. The objective is to understand how to use and extend Galleria, not how to style it beautifully.

However, while working with this theme, feel free to use additional styles to provide a custom look and feel.

Creating mobile friendly themes (Simple)

Creating mobile friendly themes will help the gallery switch seamlessly between different devices, landscape and portrait mode, and other device screen sizes. Responsive web design is a very powerful technique to style websites for various screen sizes. It allows you to provide CSS rules that are only applied when certain media queries match. Use this recipe to modify settings for Galleria to utilize responsive web techniques.

Getting ready

Before we start working on the code, we'll need to copy the basic gallery example code from the previous example and rename the folder and files to be prefixed with `mobile`. After this is done, our folder and file structure should look like the following screenshot:

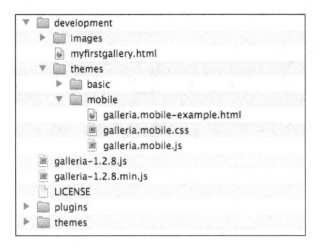

How to do it...

1. We'll start off with our `galleria.mobile.js` theme JavaScript file:

```javascript
(function($) {
Galleria.addTheme({
    name: 'mobile',
    author: 'Galleria How-to',
    css: 'galleria.mobile.css',
    defaults: {
        transition: 'fade',
        swipe: true,
        responsive: true
    },
    init: function(options) {
    }
});
}(jQuery));
```

The only difference here from our basic theme example is that we've enabled the `swipe` parameter for navigating images and the `responsive` parameter so we can use different styles for different device sizes.

2. Then, we'll provide the additional CSS file using media queries to match only smartphones. Add the following rules in the already present code in the `galleria.mobile.css` file:

```css
/* for smartphones */
@media only screen and (max-width : 480px){
    .galleria-stage, .galleria-thumbnails-container,
    .galleria-thumbnails-container, .galleria-image-nav,
    .galleria-info {
        width: 320px;
    }
    #galleria{ height: 300px; }
    .galleria-stage { max-height: 410px; }
}
```

Here, we're targeting any device size with a width less than 480 pixels. This should match smartphones in landscape and portrait mode. These styles will override the default styles when the width of the browser is less than 480 pixels.

3. Then, we wire it up just like the previous theme example. Modify the `galleria.mobile-example.html` file to include the following code snippet for bootstrapping the gallery:

```
<script>
  $(document).ready(function(){
    Galleria.loadTheme('galleria.mobile.js');
    Galleria.run('#galleria');
  });
</script>
```

We should now have a gallery that scales well for smaller device sizes, as shown in the following screenshot:

How it works...

The `responsive` option tells Galleria to actively detect screen size changes and to redraw the gallery when they are detected.

Then, our responsive CSS rules style the gallery differently for different device sizes. You can also provide additional rules so the gallery is styled differently when in portrait versus landscape mode. Galleria will detect when the device screen orientation has changed and apply the new styles accordingly.

Media queries

A very good list of media queries that can be used to target different devices for responsive web design is available at `http://css-tricks.com/snippets/css/media-queries-for-standard-devices/`.

Testing for mobile

The easiest way to test the mobile theme is to simply resize the browser window to the size of the mobile device. This simulates the mobile device screen size and allows the use of standard web development tools that modern browsers provide.

Integrating with existing sites

In order for this to work effectively with existing websites, the existing styles will also have to play nicely with mobile devices. This means that an existing site, if trying to integrate a mobile gallery, will also need to have its own styles scale correctly to mobile devices. If this is not the case and the mobile devices switch to zoom-like navigation mode for the site, the mobile gallery styles won't ever kick in.

Installing plugins (Simple)

Here we will learn how to install and utilize Galleria plugins. There are several different plugins that will allow you to enhance Galleria in many different ways.

Getting ready

Using the `myfirstgallery.html` file we created in the first section, we'll customize it to include the history plugin that is packaged with Galleria.

How to do it...

All that is required to install a plugin is to include its JavaScript file. Place the following code inside the `head` tag:

```
<script src="../galleria-1.2.8.min.js"></script>
<script src="../plugins/history/galleria.history.min.js">
</script>
<script type="text/javascript">
  $(document).ready(function(){
    Galleria.loadTheme('../themes/classic/galleria.classic.min.js');
    Galleria.run('#galleria');
  });
</script>
```

How it works...

With plugins, it's possible to hook into Galleria to customize its behavior. This ranges from customizing how Galleria retrieves its images, what images it loads, and how it handles JavaScript events.

In the case of the history plugin for image change, it adds a hash value to the URL so that each image visited in the gallery can have a unique URL. This allows users to link directly to an image inside the gallery. Then, when the page is requested with the specified hash, it will load that image instead of the initial image in the gallery and also allow the user to go backward/forward in history.

There's more...

Galleria includes three plugins in its distribution: `flickr`, `picasa`, and `history`. The `flickr` and `picasa` plugins provide an ability to view galleries directly from those photo services.

Using the Flickr plugin (Medium)

Here we will learn how we can use and extend the `flickr` plugin to display a `flickr` gallery with Galleria.

Getting ready

We're going to use the `myfirstgallery.html` file and modify the example again, though it's fine to use whatever gallery implementation is available if preferred.

How to do it...

1. Create a basic gallery with Galleria's `flickr` plugin using the following JavaScript code inside our `head` tag:

```
<script src="http://code.jquery.com/jquery.min.js"></script>
<script src="../galleria-1.2.8.min.js"></script>
<script src="../plugins/flickr/galleria.flickr.min.js">
</script>
<script type="text/javascript">
  $(document).ready(function(){
    Galleria.loadTheme(
      '../themes/classic/galleria.classic.min.js');
    Galleria.run('#galleria', {
      flickr: 'search:beach' });
  });
</script>
```

Here, we're just including the JavaScript plugin and calling the `Galleria.run` function with the flickr option to search for photos with `beach` in their title. By default, the `flickr` gallery only retrieves the first 30 Flickr photos.

2. For a more complex `flickr` gallery that continually retrieves more images from Flickr, we can use Flickr in a more dynamic way, along with Galleria, to continuously add images to the gallery as the user approaches the end of the gallery using the following code:

```
<script type="text/javascript">
$(document).ready(function(){
  Galleria.loadTheme(
        '../themes/classic/galleria.classic.min.js');
  var flickr = new Galleria.Flickr(),
      page = 1;
  flickr.search('beach', function(data) {
      Galleria.run('#galleria', { dataSource: data });
  });
  Galleria.ready(function(options) {
    var galleria = this;
    galleria.bind('loadfinish', function(e) {
      /* after an image is loaded, check to see how
         close we are to loading more images */
      if((e.index + 5) > galleria.getDataLength()){
        /* start loading more images */
        page += 1;
        flickr._find({ text: 'beach', page: page},
                    function(data) {
          // add the image data to the gallery
          galleria.push(data);
        });
      }
    });
  });
});
</script>
```

Here we're utilizing some of Galleria's API to continually add images as we approach the end of the gallery. The `loadfinish` event is called after each image is loaded. The `flickr._find` method allows us to search Flickr with a `page` parameter so that we can grab the next set of results. Finally, the `galleria.push` method lets us add the image data to the Galleria instance.

The benefit of doing it this way as opposed to loading all the images immediately is that the web page will load much faster, as it only retrieves the images as necessary.

How it works...

The `flickr` plugin uses the flickr RESTful API to retrieve images that are used with the Galleria API to dynamically add images to the gallery.

There's more...

There are additional `flickr` plugin options that can be used; however, they need to be specified in their own `flickrOptions` object:

```
Galleria.run('#galleria', {
  flickr: 'search:beach',
  flickrOptions: {
    max: 50
  }
});
```

The following list is a complete listing of `flickr` plugin options:

- `max`: This option provides the maximum number of images that will be retrieved from Flickr. Its default value is set to 30.

- `imageSize`: This option provides the size of the image. Options include small, thumb, medium, big, original. Its default value is set to medium.

- `sort`: This option provides the sort order for the images. Potential values include field followed by "asc" or "desc". Allowed fields are date-posted, date-taken, and interestingness. Its default value is set to interestingness-desc.

- `description`: This option is a Boolean to specify whether the description should also be retrieved from Flickr. Its default value is set to false.

Flickr plugin API

There is also a `flickr` plugin API that allows for more advanced behavior such as sorting, batching, group searches, and retrieving tags and set. Detailed documentation on what's available can be found at `http://galleria.io/docs/plugins/flickr/`.

Using the Flickr REST API

Additionally, Flickr provides a very robust RESTful API that the plugin utilizes. An overview on all the available methods can be found at `http://www.flickr.com/services/api/`.

The `flickr._find` method we used utilizes the `flickr.photos.search` rest method. For a more detailed description of available parameters to that method, visit `http://www.flickr.com/services/api/flickr.photos.search.html`.

Creating a plugin (Advanced)

In this recipe we'll learn how to create a plugin that retrieves images from Facebook.

Getting ready

For this exercise we're going to walk through the process of creating a Facebook plugin that will get all the public photos for the user or page provided in a Galleria option.

Before we get started, we need to create a new folder named `facebook`. Inside the folder, please create empty files with the names `galleria.facebook.js` and `galleria.facebook-example.html`.

How to do it...

Creating a plugin can include hooking into Galleria events, customizing options, or overriding Galleria methods. In the later stage, we need to make sure we still allow Galleria to function properly if the plugin isn't used, even though it might be loaded.

1. The following code with inline comments is used to create the `galleria.facebook.js` plugin:

```
(function($) {

var FACEBOOK_URL = 'https://graph.facebook.com';

/* Store the original load method so we can later call it if
   no facebook option is provided to Galleria. */
var load = Galleria.prototype.load;

/* Here we override the load method with our own that will
   check for facebook option. */
Galleria.prototype.load = function() {
  /* check if facebook option is provided. Call the
       original load if not. */
  if(typeof this._options.facebook !== 'string'){
    load.apply(this, Galleria.utils.array(arguments));
    return;
  }
}
```

```
    /* "this" in this context is the Galleria instance.
       We assign it to "galleria" so we can still have
       access to it within the context of the ajax
       callback */
    var galleria = this,
    facebook = this._options.facebook;

    $.ajax({
      /* Use the facebook graph API to get all the public
         photos for the provided facebook user or page */
      url: FACEBOOK_URL + '/' + facebook +
           '/photos?fields=picture,source&limit=50',
      /* returned data is in JSON format */
      dataType: 'json',
      success: function(data){
        var images = [];
        for(var i=0; i<data.data.length; i++){
          /* go through each image and add it to
             new images array in JSON format that
             Galleria expects */
          var _image = data.data[i];
          images.push({
            image: _image.source,
            thumb: _image.picture
          });
        }
        /* manually set the data for Galleria */
        galleria._data = images;
        /* And trigger Galleria to load with the newly
           set data */
        galleria.trigger(Galleria.DATA);
      }
    });
  };
} (jQuery));
```

2. Finally, we need to load the gallery using the plugin. For this example, we're using the "Marvel" Facebook page to retrieve images:

```
<!DOCTYPE html>
<html lang="en">
  <head>
    <script src="http://code.jquery.com/jquery.min.js"></script>
  <script src="../../galleria-1.2.8.js"></script>
```

```
<script src="galleria.facebook.js"></script>
<script>
  $(document).ready(function(){
    Galleria.loadTheme(
      '../../themes/classic/galleria.classic.min.js');
    Galleria.run('#galleria', { facebook: 'Marvel' });
  });
</script>
 </head>
 <body>
 <div id="galleria" style="height: 500px;">
 </div>
 </body>
</html>
```

Here, all we're doing differently is including the `galleria.facebook.js` file we just worked on and initializing the gallery with the facebook option. If everything worked properly, the result should be a nice gallery retrieving images from Facebook, as shown in the following screenshot:

How it works...

The plugin overrides the original load behavior of Galleria, retaining the original load behavior to fall back on if the facebook plugin is not used. Then, we use the Facebook Graph API with AJAX to retrieve the images.

What else can we do?

The possibilities for customizing Galleria are vast. In the next section, we'll be going through using the Galleria API, which will help us to understand the various places we can customize Galleria and methods we can use to dig into the Galleria framework.

Using the API (Medium)

Learn how to use the Galleria API to hook into events and use different API calls by creating a customized gallery that utilizes them.

Getting ready

For this exercise, we'll be going through an example that utilizes an event listener and API calls. To start us off, create an `api-example.html` file in the development folder.

How to do it...

1. To keep our HTML as small as possible, we'll use the `flickr` plugin. That way we don't have to reference any local images as shown in the following code:

```
<!DOCTYPE html>
<html lang="en">
<head>
 <script src="http://code.jquery.com/jquery.min.js"></script>
 <script src="../galleria-1.2.8.min.js"></script>
 <script src="../plugins/flickr/galleria.flickr.min.js">
 </script>
 <script type="text/javascript">
   $(document).ready(function(){
     Galleria.loadTheme(
       '../themes/classic/galleria.classic.min.js');
     Galleria.run('#galleria', { flickr: 'search:beach' });
   });
```

```
  </script>
 </head>
 <body>
  <div id="galleria" style="height: 500px;">
  </div>
 </body>
</html>
```

This is not any different from previous examples we worked on. Still, make sure to test out the gallery first before you proceed.

2. Next, we'll hook into Galleria's event system to temporarily show and hide the info box on the classic theme when an image is displayed. To do this we'll add the following code just below the `Galleria.run` call:

```
Galleria.ready(function(options) {
    /* show the info box when an image is displayed */
    var galleria = this;
    /* bind event when each image is displayed */
    galleria.bind('loadfinish', function(e) {
        var info = $('.galleria-info-text');
        var link = $('.galleria-info-link');
        var close = $('.galleria-info-close');
        info.fadeIn('fast');
        link.hide();
        close.show();
        setTimeout(function(){
            /* in 2 seconds, hide again */
            info.fadeOut('fast', function(){
                /* when the info box is completely hidden,
                   we can then toggle the link and close
                   buttons. */
                link.show();
                close.hide();
            });
        }, 2000);
    });
});
```

The `Galleria.ready` function runs the code provided in the anonymous function after the gallery is set up. Then, the `bind` method is used on the galleria instance to bind events just as in jQuery. Here, the `loadfinish` event is triggered every time after an image is loaded into the gallery. The anonymous function provided as the final parameter takes only one parameter, an event object. That one event object provides information on the particular event and the state of the gallery. Then, inside the event handler, we're simply retrieving the info element, fading it in so it can be seen, and then setting a timer to fade out.

3. Next, we're going to provide a pause/play button for the gallery. This won't require any event handlers, just adding elements to the DOM and utilizing Galleria's API. We'll add the following code below the previous event handler code:

```
Galleria.ready(function(options) {
    var galleria = this;
    /* Add pause/play button to DOM */
    var pauseplay = $('<div class="pauseplay" />').
                            insertAfter('.galleria-counter');
    /* Check if auto play specified. If it is, we know
       the gallery is playing already */
    if(galleria._options.autoplay){
        pauseplay.addClass('playing').html('pause');
    }else{
        pauseplay.html('play');
    }
    /* Handle click events on the button to start/stop playing
       the gallery and to change the text for the button */
    pauseplay.click(function(){
        if(pauseplay.hasClass('playing')){
            galleria.pause();
            pauseplay.html('play').removeClass('playing');
        ''}else{
            galleria.play();
            pauseplay.addClass('playing').html('pause');
        }
    });
});
```

Here, we are first looking to see if `autoplay` is enabled so we know if the gallery is already playing. To do this, we look at the provided options for Galleria: `galleria._options.autoplay`. Then, Galleria provides simple pause and play methods as part of its API.

4. To style the pause/play button, place the following code below the script tag we're working in:

```
<style>
    .pauseplay{
        position: absolute;
        bottom: 10px;
        left: 45px;
        background-color: #EBEBEB;
```

```
        font: normal 11px/1 arial,sans-serif;
        color: black;
        z-index: 1;
        cursor: pointer;
        padding: 2px;
    }
</style>
```

Here, we're just placing the button to the right of the counter and styling it so it's somewhat noticeable.

5. Lastly, let's go through opening a lightbox of the gallery using the following code:

```
Galleria.ready(function(options) {
    var galleria = this;
    var button = $('<div class="lightbox-btn">Light Box</div>').
        insertAfter('.galleria-counter');
    button.click(function(){
        galleria.openLightbox();
    });
});
```

All we're doing here is adding a lightbox button and using the `galleria.openLightbox` method to open the Galleria lightbox when the button is clicked.

6. To style the lightbox use the following code:

```
<style>
    .lightbox-btn{
        position: absolute;
        bottom: 10px;
        right: 30px;
        background-color: #EBEBEB;
        font: normal 11px/1 arial,sans-serif;
        color: black;
        z-index: 1;
        cursor: pointer;
        padding: 2px;
    }
</style>
```

There's more...

The following list provides a quick reference to useful Galleria events:

- `thumbnail`: This event triggers when a thumbnail is displayed.
- `loadstart`: This event triggers when an image has begun loading in the gallery.
- `loadfinish`: This event triggers when an image has finished loading in the gallery.
- `image`: This event triggers when an image is displayed and finished its transition.
- `play`: This event triggers when a gallery starts playing.
- `pause`: This event triggers when a gallery is paused.
- `idle_enter`: This event triggers when a gallery is placed into idle mode. Idle mode is when the user does not interact with the gallery for the configured set of milliseconds.
- `idle_exit`: This event triggers when a gallery leaves idle mode.
- `rescale`: This event triggers when a gallery is rescaled.

The following list provides a quick reference for useful Galleria API methods:

- `play`: This method is used to start playing the gallery
- `pause`: This method is used to pause the gallery
- `next`: This method is used to go to the next image in the gallery
- `prev`: This method is used to go to the previous image in the gallery
- `show(index)`: This method shows the image of the specified index
- `openLightbox`: This method opens the lightbox for the current image
- `load`: This method loads new image data
- `push`: This method adds additional image data to the gallery
- `setOptions`: This method sets gallery options
- `getActiveImage`: This method gets the image that is currently displayed

Complete API reference

A complete reference to all API methods is available at `http://galleria.io/docs/api/methods/` and for a complete list of all events visit `http://galleria.io/docs/api/events/`.

Another way to bind events

Instead of placing the event binding inside a `Galleria.ready` call, we can use the `Galleria.on` function if you prefer the following syntactical style:

```
Galleria.on('mygalleriaevent', function(e){
   /* event code */
});
```

Alternative image data structures (Simple)

This recipe provides an overview of the various methods used to provide alternative data structures for the Galleria framework to consume.

Getting ready

The data used to display images and other media for a gallery has a number of attributes that can be set up. Typically, Galleria just finds relevant image URLs, title, and description for the image and displays the gallery with that; however, there are more options possible to create a more robust gallery than what is typically used.

The full list of available image properties that can be set through HTML data attributes (HTML tag attributes that begin with `data-`) or JavaScript is as follows:

- `thumb`: This property provides the thumbnail image
- `image`: This property provides the main image (required)
- `big`: This property provides the big image for fullscreen mode
- `title`: This property provides the image title
- `description`: This property provides the image description
- `link`: This property provides the image URL link
- `layer`: This property provides a layer of HTML that will be displayed on top of the content
- `video`: This property provides a URL to a video; as of Version 1.2.7 we support Vimeo, Youtube, and Dailymotion URLs
- `iframe`: This property provides a URL to be displayed in an iframe
- `original`: This property provides a reference to the original `IMG` element

Full documentation covering image properties can be found via Galleria's website at `http://galleria.io/docs/references/data/`.

Before we start using the different image data properties, we'll create a file in the development folder called `data-structures.html`. To start off, we'll create the basic HTML structure for our gallery using the following code:

```html
<!DOCTYPE html>
<html lang="en">
  <head>
    <script src="http://code.jquery.com/jquery.min.js">
    </script>
    <script src="../galleria-1.2.8.min.js"></script>
    <script>
      // Galleria initialization will be placed here
    </script>
  </head>
<body>
  <div id="galleria" style="height: 500px;">
    <!-- html image structure will be placed here -->
  </div>
</body>
</html>
```

Specifying extra parameters via IMG tag

The usual HTML structure for image data is to provide an `anchor` tag linking to the image displayed in the gallery, which then wraps an `img` tag that specifies the thumbnail and additional image properties for the gallery.

The following code is an example of this in practice:

```html
<div id="galleria-img-tag" style="height: 500px;">
  <!-- anchor tag wrapping img tag -->
  <a href="images/image1-1600px.jpg">
    <img data-title="Image 1"
         data-description="Image 1 description"
         src="images/image1-200px.jpg"
         data-link="images/image1-1600px.jpg" />
  </a>
  <!-- More images defined in this way -->
</div>
```

This code will be initialized with the following JavaScript code:

```
<script>
  $(document).ready(function(){
    Galleria.loadTheme(
      '../themes/classic/galleria.classic.min.js');
    Galleria.run('#galleria-img-tag');
  });
</script>
```

Galleria understands `data-` prefixed attributes as settings for Galleria on that image. So `data-title`, `data-description`, and `data-link` are all Galleria image properties that are set via HTML data attributes. Additional properties could be provided here such as `data-big` or `data-original`.

Alternative media

In addition to images, Galleria can also display video and iframes inside the gallery. The method by which this is accomplished is mostly the same as the way images are specified, with the only difference being that the image URL is replaced with the video or iframe URL. Galleria supports YouTube, Vimeo, and Dailymotion video URLs.

The following code is an example of adding just a YouTube video:

```
<div id="galleria-media" style="height: 500px;">
  <a href="http://www.youtube.com/watch?v=8gSPbmgWr_Y">
    <img data-title="Youtube video"
         data-description="Youtube description"
        src="http://i3.ytimg.com/i/vC4D8onUfXzvjTOM-dBfEA/1.
jpg?v=50aaaeea"
        data-link="http://www.youtube.com/watch?v=8gSPbmgWr_Y" />
  </a>
</div>
```

This code should be initialized with the following JavaScript code:

```
<script>
  $(document).ready(function(){
    Galleria.loadTheme('../themes/classic/galleria.classic.min.js');
    Galleria.run('#galleria-media');
  });
</script>
```

As we can see, the HTML structure is basically identical. The only difference here is that we're using a YouTube video URL instead of an image URL.

Using JSON

It's also possible to use JSON data to initialize Galleria. This is useful when we want to initialize Galleria programmatically with JavaScript or when the image data is gathered on a remote server.

In our example, we'll load the same images as previously, just with a JSON structure instead of HTML, using the following code:

```
<script>
$(document).ready(function(){
    Galleria.loadTheme(
        '../themes/classic/galleria.classic.min.js');
    var data = [
        {
            thumb: 'images/image1-200px.jpg',
            image: 'images/image1-1600px.jpg',
            title: 'Image 1',
            description: 'Image 1 description'
        },{
            thumb: 'images/image2-200px.jpg',
            image: 'images/image2-1600px.jpg',
            title: 'Image 2',
            description: 'Image 2 description'
        }];
    Galleria.run('#galleria-json', {
        dataSource: data });
});
</script>
```

Here, we're just using the `dataSource` property to specify an array of images that Galleria will use for the gallery.

HTML structure parsing customization

It's possible that you'll have an existing HTML markup that doesn't fit in the HTML pattern that Galleria expects. Here, we'll look into customizing how Galleria gathers the image properties for the gallery from the DOM.

For example, if working with a definition list (dl) of images, titles, and descriptions, all the required properties are available in order to create a gallery.

```
<div id="galleria-dataconfig" style="height: 500px;">
  <dl>
    <dt><img src="images/image1-1600px.jpg"
             data-thumb="images/image1-200px.jpg" />
    </dt>
```

```
<dd>
  <span class="title">Image 1</span>
  <span class="description">Image 1 Description</span>
</dd>
<dt><img src="images/image2-1600px.jpg"
        data-thumb="images/image2-200px.jpg"/>
</dt>
<dd>
  <span class="title">Image 2</span>
  <span class="description">Image 2 Description</span>
</dd>
  </dl>
</div>
```

All that's left is instructing Galleria how to gather those properties from the DOM, which can be done with the following JavaScript code:

```
$(document).ready(function(){
    Galleria.loadTheme(
      '../themes/classic/galleria.classic.min.js');
    Galleria.run('#galleria-dataconfig', {
        dataConfig: function(img) {
            var img = $(img);
            return {
                thumb: img.data('thumb'),
                title: img.parent().next().
                        find('.title').html(),
                description: img.parent().next().
                        find('.description').html()
            }
        }
    });
});
```

What is being done here is that Galleria is finding every instance of an `img` tag and passing it into the provided `dataConfig` function, which then returns the rest of the image properties via simple jQuery DOM traversal.

How it works...

Before an image is displayed in a gallery, Galleria uses the various methods we described previously to parse image data so that it can easily be customized.

Optimizing Galleria (Simple)

This recipe discusses optimizing Galleria by using various methods that help to improve the performance of Galleria.

Getting ready

Since this recipe is just discussing various techniques to improve the performance of Galleria, we'll not use a specific example to walk through. The following techniques can be applied to any of the galleries created throughout the book.

Image sizes

For images deployed to a website, always use sizes complementary to the size of the gallery. If the image is drastically larger than the gallery, a visitor to the site will be downloading larger images than what is necessary and this can slow down the performance.

Providing thumbnails

Always provide thumbnails for galleries as we've done so far in this book. Thumbnails are much smaller versions of the original images that are shown in the carousel. Galleria will only preload (a parameter that can be customized) a couple of non-thumbnail images ahead of time; however, if no thumbnail is provided, all of the larger images will be loaded since the thumbnails will always be shown.

The ideal thumbnail size will depend on the size utilized in the theme.

Optimizing resources

Always use minified versions of JavaScript and CSS resources on live sites so visitors are only required to download the smaller version of the files. A minified version of a resource is one where the contents of the file are optimized for small file sizes. Galleria ships with minified versions of all its resources—these are resources with filenames that end with `.min.js` or `.min.css`.

In addition, merge multiple JavaScript and CSS resources into single files. The advantage of this is that a site visitor has fewer requests to make for resources before it can finish rendering a page.

Some CMS platforms, such as Plone, will provide this merging and minification automatically. So if you are developing in those platforms, make sure CSS and dependent JavaScript resources are merged along with the rest of the site's resources.

Galleria size

For dynamically loading Galleria images, it is not advised to create large galleries (those over 30 images). Especially for non-modern browsers, this can affect performance. In the following recipe, we'll discuss how to dynamically load more images as the gallery is being browsed.

Web server

Modern web servers provide features that help improve website performance. For example, make sure to enable compression on assets being delivered by your web application. Most web servers, for example Nginx and Apache, support gzip compression by default. In addition, make sure to configure your web server to set appropriate cache headers.

Resource minification

There are free online tools for minifying resources to use if minification is not provided on the utilized platform. For CSS, tools are available at `http://www.minifycss.com/`. For JavaScript, tools are available at `http://www.minifyjavascript.com/`.

Adding images dynamically (Medium)

Learn how to dynamically add images to galleries via triggered web page events or while a user navigates through a gallery so that images are loaded lazily. Loading images lazily can improve the performance and usability of your gallery.

Getting ready

For this example, we're going to assume all our images are located in a single directory and follow specific naming conventions. This allows us to dynamically load more images according to those conventions.

To start out, we'll create a file in our `development` directory named `dynamic-images.html` with the contents as shown in the following code:

```html
<!DOCTYPE html>
<html lang="en">
  <head>
    <script src="http://code.jquery.com/jquery.min.js">
    </script>
    <script src="../galleria-1.2.8.min.js"></script>
    <script type="text/javascript">
      /* Galleria initialization code */
    </script>
  </head>
  <body>
    <div id="galleria" style="height: 500px;">
    </div>
  </body>
</html>
```

This will just provide us with the basic structure before we start writing our JavaScript code.

How to do it...

The following process of dynamically loading more images in a gallery is simple:

1. First, create a JavaScript method that will retrieve the additional images.
2. Next, bind the `loadstart` Galleria event so that we can check every time a new image is loaded, if it's time to add more images to the gallery.
3. Lastly, in the `loadstart` event handler, provide the correct logic to decide if more images can be loaded.

Here is a sample JavaScript snippet that will provide what was just discussed:

```javascript
<script>
    /* function to get images with URLs generated
       from one number to another larger number */
    var getImages = function(from, to){
        var data = [];
        for(var i=from; i<=to; i++){
            data.push({
                image: 'images/image' + i + '-1600px.jpg',
                thumb: 'images/image' + i + '-200px.jpg',
                title: 'Image ' + i,
                description: 'Image ' + i + ' Description'
            });
```

```
        }
        return data;
    }
    $(document).ready(function(){
        Galleria.loadTheme(
            '../themes/classic/galleria.classic.min.js');
        /* Load with the first 2 images */
        Galleria.run('#galleria', {
            dataSource: getImages(1, 2),
        });
        Galleria.ready(function(options) {
            var galleria = this;
            galleria.bind('loadstart', function(e) {
                /* after an image starts load, check to see
                   how close we are to loading more images */
                var size = galleria.getDataLength();
                if((e.index + 2) > size && size <= 10){
                    galleria.push(
                        getImages(size + 1,
                            Math.min(size + 2, 10)));
                }
            })
        });
    });
</script>
```

The `getImages` method is designed to retrieve a section of the 10 available images on the filesystem. The `dataSource` Galleria parameter is used to load the initial couple of images in Galleria. Finally, we bind the `loadstart` event, and inside it we add more images to Galleria with the `galleria.push` method if more images are available.

How it works...

Since we know the naming convention of the images on the filesystem, we can dynamically construct the necessary image URLs for the gallery. In addition, Galleria provides the necessary events and API calls for us to be able to hook in and dynamically load images.

Following up with server-side techniques

We can also combine this technique with an AJAX request to a web server that returns additional image data from server side code. The server could potentially have image data that knows about images for the gallery stored so that a specific naming convention wouldn't be required.

Triggering Galleria (Advanced)

This recipe discusses loading Galleria and changing images from different webpage events.

Getting ready

Sometimes it's required to delay loading Galleria until sometime after a page is rendered. Additionally, you may want to trigger displaying a specific image in the gallery with an event outside the gallery. With this recipe, we'll configure Galleria to be loaded only when a user decides to view the gallery and images to be shown when a user performs a specific action outside of the gallery.

To get us started, create a file named `trigger-exampe.html` in the development directory we've been working in with the following structure:

```html
<!DOCTYPE html>
<html lang="en">
  <head>
    <script src="http://code.jquery.com/jquery.min.js">
    </script>
    <script src="../galleria-1.2.8.min.js"></script>
    <script>
      /* Galleria initialization */
    </script>
  </head>
  <body>
    <div id="galleria"
         style="height: 500px; display: none">
      <!-- supply images here -->
    </div>
    <a id="show-gallery">Show Gallery</a> |
    <a id="show-image">Show Image 2</a>
  </body>
</html>
```

Make sure to fill in the image HTML structure to test with. We'll fill in the Galleria JavaScript initialization code in the following example.

How to do it...

To accomplish this, we'll add event handlers for click events on the anchor tags to "Show Gallery" and "Show Image 2".

```
<script>
  $(document).ready(function(){
    /* when the element with the id "show-gallery" is clicked,
       create the gallery. */
    $('#show-gallery').click(function(e){
      $(this).remove();
      $('#galleria').show();
      Galleria.loadTheme(
        '../themes/classic/galleria.classic.min.js');
      Galleria.run('#galleria');
      /* prevent the default link behaviour */
      e.preventDefault();
    });
    $('#show-image').click(function(e){
      var galleria = Galleria.get(0);
      if(galleria === undefined){
        alert('Galleria not initialized yet.');
      }else{
        galleria.show(1);
      }
      e.preventDefault();
    });
  });
</script>
```

Here, we register `click` event handlers for each of the anchor tags we added to the document. Rendering the gallery inside a click event is identical to registering as we have been doing throughout the book. Here, we're just doing the same inside the click event.

To show an image on a `click` event outside the gallery, we use `Galleria.get` to retrieve the current active Galleria instance active on the page. Then we use the `galleria.show` method to show the second image of the gallery.

How it works...

Galleria initialization is done with JavaScript so that it can be initialized in any number of ways. In our example, it was just a simple click event; however, any number of scenarios can be devised to destroy existing gallery instances and recreate new instances with events.

Recording image views with Google Analytics (Medium)

This recipe discusses how to track which images are viewed with Google Analytics.

Getting ready

To get us started, we create a new `ga-example.html` file inside our `development` directory. Include a couple of sample images so that we can inspect the Google Analytics tracking requests being sent.

The basic HTML structure will look like the following code snippet with the normal Google Analytics code at the bottom of the file:

```
<!DOCTYPE html>
<html lang="en">
  <head>
    <script src="http://code.jquery.com/jquery.min.js">
    </script>
    <script src="../galleria-1.2.8.min.js"></script>
    <script>
      /* Galleria initialization */
    </script>
  </head>
  <body>
    <!-- Galleria HTML definition -->
    <div id="galleria" style="height: 500px;">
      <a href="images/image1-1600px.jpg">
        <img data-title="Image 1"
             data-description="Image 1 description"
             src="images/image1-200px.jpg"
             data-link="images/image1-1600px.jpg" />
      </a>
      <a href="images/image2-1600px.jpg">
        <img data-title="Image 2"
             data-description="Image 2 description"
             src="images/image2-200px.jpg"
             data-link="images/image2-1600px.jpg" />
      </a>
    </div>
    <script>
```

```
/* Standard analytic JavaScript source. Please replace
   "<CODE>" with your GA code */
var _gaq = _gaq || [];
_gaq.push(['_setAccount', '<CODE>']);
_gaq.push(['_trackPageview']);
(function() {
  var ga = document.createElement('script');
  ga.type = 'text/javascript'; ga.async = true;
  ga.src = ('https:' == document.location.protocol ?
            'https://ssl' : 'http://www') +
           '.google-analytics.com/ga.js';
  var s = document.getElementsByTagName('script')[0];
  s.parentNode.insertBefore(ga, s);
})();
    </script>
  </body>
</html>
```

How to do it...

The Google Analytics JavaScript includes an API to push page tracking manually to Google. In our case, we'll hook into a Galleria image view event and send out a Google Analytics page tracker request. The Google Analytics JavaScript API uses AJAX to send out the tracker request so a new page load isn't required.

```
<script>
  $(document).ready(function(){
    Galleria.loadTheme(
      '../themes/classic/galleria.classic.min.js');
    Galleria.run('#galleria');
    Galleria.ready(function(options) {
      var galleria = this;
      galleria.bind('loadstart', function(e) {
        var url = e.imageTarget.src;
        var host = window.location.hostname;
        _gaq.push(['_setCustomVar', 1,
                   "galleryView", "yes", 1]);
        _gaq.push(['_trackPageview',
                   url.substring(url.indexOf(host) +
                                 host.length)]);
      });
    });
  });
</script>
```

The code pattern here follows much of what has been done throughout the book. We're registering an event handler that'll fire when a new image is shown in the gallery. Then, we're sending the tracker request to the Google Analytics API. We make sure to only get the full path of the image to track in Google Analytics. The host name is not allowed.

How it works...

The Google Analytics API provides an API to push page tracking to it manually in JavaScript. We're just utilizing that API in this example with basic Galleria API programming.

There's more...

Google Analytics has a robust JavaScript API if there is a need to do something more fancy. Check out their documentation available at `https://developers.google.com/analytics/devguides/collection/gajs/methods/`.

Handling errors gracefully (Medium)

If certain images cannot be loaded, handle it in a graceful way so users aren't confronted with a broken, ugly gallery.

Getting ready

There are two types of Galleria errors, fatal, and warnings. Fatal errors will throw a JavaScript exception and stop all following JavaScript from running. Warnings will cause Galleria to not show an image and then present an error box to the user.

Fatal errors can result from the following reasons:

- ▶ Not being able to load the theme file
- ▶ Not finding that target HTML element to create the gallery
- ▶ Hitting the browser stylesheet limit (Internet Explorer related)
- ▶ Not finding the theme
- ▶ Not determining gallery width and height
- ▶ Width or height is too small for displaying gallery

Warnings can result from the following:

- Another gallery instance already running
- HTML running in quirks mode
- Failing to load image data
- Not extracting width and height from image
- Not finding an image
- Not being able to scale an image

We'll use two separate methods to handle each of these types of errors in Galleria to help handle them better.

To implement our error handlers, let's create a file named `errors-example.html` in the `development` directory. The contents can be a very basic Galleria setup as follows:

```html
<!DOCTYPE html>
<html lang="en">
  <head>
    <script src="http://code.jquery.com/jquery.min.js">
    </script>
    <script src="../galleria-1.2.8.min.js"></script>
    <script>
      $(document).ready(function(){
        Galleria.loadTheme(
          '../themes/classic/galleria.classic.min.js');
        Galleria.run('#galleria');
      });
    </script>
  </head>
  <body>
    <div id="galleri1a" style="height: 500px;">
      <a href="images/image1-1600px.jpg">
        <img data-title="Image 1"
             data-description="Image 1 description"
             src="images/image1-200px.jpg"
             data-link="images/image1-1600px.jpg" />
      </a>
      <!-- other images -->
    </div>
  </body>
</html>
```

How to do it...

Since fatal errors prevent other JavaScript from executing on the page, it's especially important that we handle these errors. In addition, it's important to give the user an indication that the Galleria failed to load.

As for warnings, they'll most likely be caused by incorrect configuration but there are still ways to prevent them from being too much of a nuisance.

To override the default error handling strategy, let's work through the following code:

```
<script>
  $(document).ready(function(){
    Galleria.loadTheme(
      '../themes/classic/galleria.classic.min.js');
    Galleria.run('#galleria', {
      debug: false,
      dummy: 'images/dummy.jpg'
    });
  });
</script>
```

How it works...

Setting `debug` to `false` prevents Galleria from throwing a JavaScript fatal error and stopping the execution of any additional JavaScript. In addition, setting a `dummy` image tells Galleria to use that image instead of showing an error message or failing when an image fails to load.

Creating tests for customizations (Advanced)

This recipe creates tests for Galleria customizations that can be run across many browsers. This will allow you to ensure the quality of your customizations via automated testing.

Getting ready

In the tests we're going to write, we'll be using the Selenium test framework with the Firefox web browser. The advantage of Selenium is that it comes with an IDE plugin so novices can even write tests. The difficultly level is ideal to cover in this book.

We'll be using Selenium to record user interactions with our Galleria customizations. Once these interactions are recorded, they can then be tested against any additional functionality or changes to ensure that everything is still working as expected.

Before we get started, please download the Firefox web browser if you have not already done so, available at `http://www.mozilla.org/firefox`. Follow the instructions to download and install.

Then, open Firefox and visit `http://seleniumhq.org/download/` and follow the instructions to download and install the Firefox Selenium IDE plugin. Make sure to restart Firefox after the plugin is installed.

Finally, open up Selenium IDE by clicking on **Tools** in the menu bar and then selecting the `Selenium IDE` item in the menu. There should be a Selenium IDE window like the one in the following screenshot:

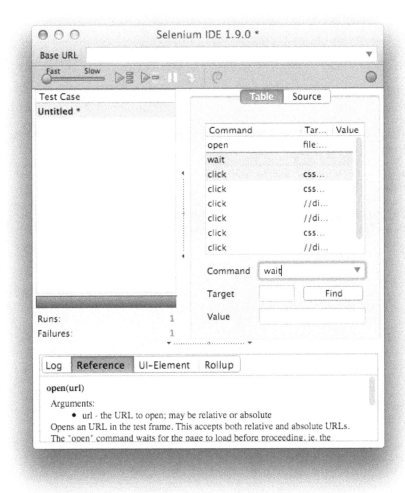

Once Selenium is set up, locate the `myfirstgallery.html` file that we created in the *Setting up the development environment* recipe. We'll be creating tests for that gallery.

How to do it...

1. First, open the `myfirstgallery.html` file in Firefox.

2. Then, click on the record button (red button in the upper right-hand corner) and then start using the gallery as the user would. Selenium will be recording all the actions that we perform.

3. Once all the functionality is tested, click on the record button once more to stop recording.

4. Now, before we run the test just created, reduce the speed all the way down. It should look like the following screenshot:

Modifying this prevents Selenium from running the test action too quickly. If it ran too quickly, Galleria wouldn't finish the transitions before the next action is performed.

5. Finally, click the play button to run the test we just recorded. The whole test suite should run without failure if it was done correctly.

6. Inspect the source tab of the recorded test. It should contain something similar to the following code snippet:

```
<?xml version="1.0" encoding="UTF-8"?>
<!DOCTYPE html PUBLIC "-//W3C//DTD XHTML 1.0 Strict//EN" "http://
www.w3.org/TR/xhtml1/DTD/xhtml1-strict.dtd">
<html xmlns="http://www.w3.org/1999/xhtml" xml:lang="en"
lang="en">
<head profile="http://selenium-ide.openqa.org/profiles/test-case">
<meta http-equiv="Content-Type" content="text/html; charset=UTF-8"
/>
<link rel="selenium.base" href="http://change-this-to-the-site-
you-are-testing/" />
<title>New Test</title>
</head>
<body>
<!-- Each test is specified in table format.
     Each row specifies an action the Selenium is
     automating -->
<table cellpadding="1" cellspacing="1" border="1">
 <thead>
  <tr><td rowspan="1" colspan="3">New Test</td></tr>
 </thead>
 <tbody>
```

```
    <tr>
        <td>open</td>
<td>file:///path/to/galleria/development/myfirstgallery.html</td>
        <td></td>
    </tr>
    <tr>
    <td>click</td>
    <td>css=div.galleria-image-nav-right</td>
    <td></td>
    </tr>
    <tr>
    <td>click</td>
    <td>css=div.galleria-image-nav-right</td>
    <td></td>
    </tr>
    <tr>
    <td>click</td>
    <td>css=div.galleria-image-nav-right</td>
    <td></td>
    </tr>
<!-- more tests would follow →
</tbody></table>
</body>
</html>
```

The test code is actually just simple HTML table markup with events and element selectors, so from here it's possible to save these tests as files to version control and run them on different machines and browsers.

In addition to the actions that were recorded, it would be beneficial to also include assert statements to make sure certain elements are present in the DOM as each action is performed. Inspect Selenium IDE for details on using more commands and tests.

How it works...

Selenium IDE allows us to record all the actions being performed in the browser. Then the Selenium test driver plays the tests defined against a web browser, in our case Firefox.

Those tests can be run against a Selenium server that is set up to test against multiple browsers and operating systems.

Read more about the selenium testing framework

Selenium has a vast API and documentation area on its website. Anyone who is interested in learning more about it should read it, available at `http://seleniumhq.org/`.

Web application integration (Advanced)

Integrate Galleria with a web application platform or CMS. In this recipe, we'll cover creating a web application that reads images from a filesystem directory.

Getting ready

For the sake of this example, we'll be introducing a new programming language and platform to work with. The purpose is to show how a possible web application integration would work. We'll be using the Python programming language and the Flask web application framework. Both are known for their ease of use so hopefully it'll be easy to understand for someone that has no experience with the technologies. It's fine to skip the following paragraphs if there is no interest in learning the Python tools used here.

Before we start, install Python. We'll be using Python 2.7 in this example. Please visit `http://www.python.org/getit/` for information on installing. Command line examples will be given for both Unix Bash and Windows.

Once Python is installed, enter the following command in the `cmd.exe` application (Windows):

```
C:\Python27\Scripts\easy_install.exe Flask
```

Enter the following command for Unix:

```
sudo easy_install Flask
```

Next, create files named `app.py` and `app.html` in the `development` directory we've been working in. We'll use those files for the web application we'll write.

How to do it...

In our sample Flask web application, we're going to dynamically read images from the filesystem to create our gallery with and use a templating engine to generate the HTML markup required for the gallery. Here, we're using a templating engine to dynamically render HTML markup. Previously, the HTML markup we used was manually crafted.

Since the following code snippet is a bit longer, please read the inline comments. The contents of `app.py` will look like the following:

```python
import os
from flask import Flask, render_template

# Create the application
app = Flask('Galleria', static_folder="../",
```

```
            static_url_path="/static", template_folder="./")

    # Set the directory where images are stored
    image_dir = os.path.join(os.path.dirname(__file__), 'images')


@app.route("/")
def index():
    """
    Run this function for the index page of the web application.

    Images on the filesystem are expected to be in the format for
    thumbnails:
        image#-200px.jpg

    And this format for large size:
        image#-1600px.jpg
    """
    images = {}
    for filename in os.listdir(image_dir):
        # if the filename does not start with image,
        # it's not a valid gallery image
        if not filename.startswith('image'):
            continue

        # let's find the scale size
        name, size = filename.split('-')
        if name not in images:
            images[name] = {}
        if size.startswith('200px'):
            # thumbnail
            images[name]['thumb'] = filename
        else:
            # full size
            images[name]['image'] = filename
    # render the app.html template with the image data we gathered
    return render_template('app.html', images=images.values())

if __name__ == "__main__":
    app.run()
```

Here we're setting up the Flask app and setting up one URL—the index page of the site. What the index page of the site shows depends on what is returned in the function we have defined. In our case, we're rendering a template with the values of the images we found on the filesystem.

The `app.html` file will then look like the following code:

```html
<!DOCTYPE html>
<html lang="en">
  <head>
    <script src="http://code.jquery.com/jquery.min.js">
    </script>
    <script src="/static/galleria-1.2.8.min.js"></script>
    <script>
      $(document).ready(function(){
        Galleria.loadTheme(
          '/static/themes/classic/galleria.classic.min.js');
        Galleria.run('#galleria');
      });
    </script>
  </head>
<body>
  <div id="galleria" style="height: 500px;">
    {% for image in images %}
      <a href="/static/development/images/{{ image['image'] }}">
        <img src="/static/development/images/{{ image['thumb'] }}" />
      </a>
    {% endfor %}
  </div>
</body>
</html>
```

The important part of this HTML code is bolded. We're iterating over the set of images provided to the template and rendering the new image URL as the web application knows it.

Finally, to run the application, in the command line, move to the directory where the `app.py` file is located:

```
cd galleria/development
```

Then, run the following command to start up the web application (Windows):

```
C:\Python27\python.exe app.py
```

Run the following command to start up the web application (Unix):

```
python app.py
```

We should get the following output, letting us know that the Flask app is running correctly:

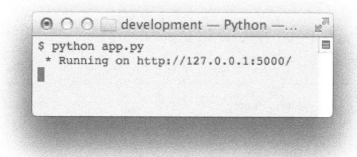

Finally, in a web browser, enter the address: `http://127.0.0.1:5000/`.

If all went well, we should see a gallery with the classic theme on the page.

How it works...

This example works much like the rest of the Galleria example with the exception of the image HTML markup being generated by Python code and the JavaScript, CSS, and images resources being served by the web application.

The advantage of using a web application is that the images used can be dynamically generated. With our application, we could simply add photos to the images directory, also naming them according to the standard we're using, and the gallery will automatically begin using those images.

Automatic thumbnail generation

Many web application frameworks and CMSs provide ways to automatically scale images for thumbnail and other sizes. If programming in those environments, please be aware of what those technologies are and make sure to utilize them accordingly.

For instance, with our example, we could use the **Python Image Library** (**PIL**) to dynamically resize our large images for use in the gallery.

Existing application Galleria integrations

Some CMSs already provide Galleria integration as follows:

- ▶ Plone: This is the Python based enterprise level CMS
  - ❏ addon: `http://plone.org/products/plone-true-gallery`
- ▶ Wordpress: This is the blogging platform
  - ❏ addon: `http://wordpress.org/extend/plugins/photo-galleria/`
- ▶ Joomla: This is the PHP CMS

  - ❏ addon: `http://www.joohopia.com/joomla-modules/jgalleria-module.html`

Search the addons of other platforms for Galleria to see if it's supported.

Thank you for buying
Instant Galleria How-to

About Packt Publishing

Packt, pronounced 'packed', published its first book *"Mastering phpMyAdmin for Effective MySQL Management"* in April 2004 and subsequently continued to specialize in publishing highly focused books on specific technologies and solutions.

Our books and publications share the experiences of your fellow IT professionals in adapting and customizing today's systems, applications, and frameworks. Our solution based books give you the knowledge and power to customize the software and technologies you're using to get the job done. Packt books are more specific and less general than the IT books you have seen in the past. Our unique business model allows us to bring you more focused information, giving you more of what you need to know, and less of what you don't.

Packt is a modern, yet unique publishing company, which focuses on producing quality, cutting-edge books for communities of developers, administrators, and newbies alike. For more information, please visit our website: www.packtpub.com.

Writing for Packt

We welcome all inquiries from people who are interested in authoring. Book proposals should be sent to author@packtpub.com. If your book idea is still at an early stage and you would like to discuss it first before writing a formal book proposal, contact us; one of our commissioning editors will get in touch with you.

We're not just looking for published authors; if you have strong technical skills but no writing experience, our experienced editors can help you develop a writing career, or simply get some additional reward for your expertise.

PACKT
PUBLISHING

Quick answers to common problems

**Ext JS 4 Web Application
Development Cookbook**

Over 110 easy-to-follow recipes backed up with real-life
examples, walking you through basic Ext JS features to
advanced application design using Sencha's Ext JS

Stuart Ashworth   Andrew Duncan   [   ] open source

Ext JS 4 Web Application Development Cookbook

ISBN: 978-1-849516-86-0   Paperback: 488 pages

Over 110 easy-to-follow recipes backed up with real-life
examples, walking you through basic Ext JS features to
advanced application design using Sencha's Ext JS

1. Learn how to build Rich Internet Applications
    with the latest version of the Ext JS framework
    in a cookbook style

2. From creating forms to theming your interface,
    you will learn the building blocks for developing
    the perfect web application

3. Easy to follow recipes step through practical and
    detailed examples which are all fully backed up
    with code, illustrations, and tips

Learning Ext JS 4

Sencha Ext JS for a beginner

Crysfel Villa
Armando Gonzalez   PACKT open source

Learning Ext JS 4

ISBN: 978-1-849516-84-6   Paperback: 434 pages

Sencha Ext JS for a beginner

1. Learn the basics and create your first classes

2. Handle data and understand the way it works,
    create powerful widgets and new components

3. Dig into the new architecture defined by Sencha
    and work on real world projects

Please check **www.PacktPub.com** for information on our titles

Learning jQuery, Third Edition

ISBN: 978-1-849516-54-9   Paperback: 428 pages

Create better interaction, design, and web development with simple JavaScript techniques

1. An introduction to jQuery that requires minimal programming experience

2. Detailed solutions to specific client-side problems

3. Revised and updated version of this popular jQuery book

jQuery 1.4 Reference Guide

ISBN: 978-1-849510-04-2   Paperback: 336 pages

A comprehensive exploration of the popular JavaScript library

1. Quickly look up features of the jQuery library

2. Step through each function, method, and selector expression in the jQuery library with an easy-to-follow approach

3. Write your own plug-ins using jQuery's powerful plug-in architecture

Please check **www.PacktPub.com** for information on our titles

www.ingramcontent.com/pod-product-compliance
Lightning Source LLC
LaVergne TN
LVHW080104070326
832902LV00014B/2418